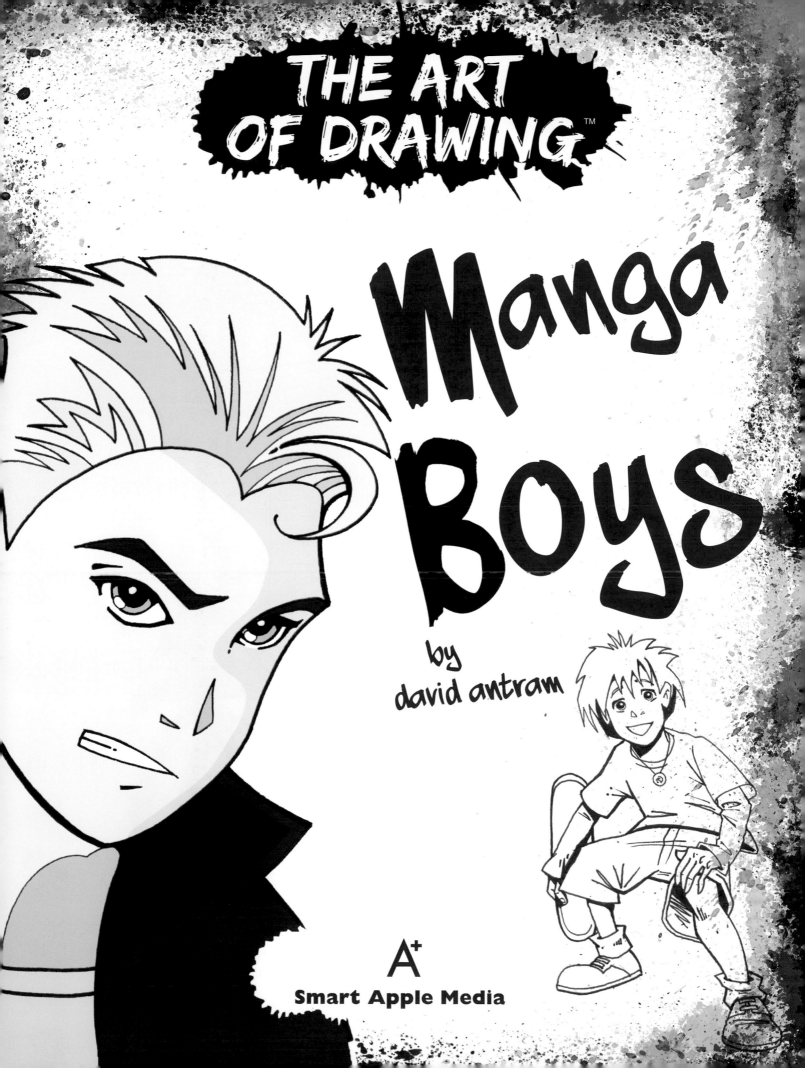

Published by Smart Apple Media,
an imprint of Black Rabbit Books
P.O. Box 3263, Mankato, Minnesota 56002
www.blackrabbitbooks.com

Published by arrangement with
The Salariya Book Company Ltd

Cataloging-in-Publication Data is available
from the Library of Congress

Printed in the United States
At Corporate Graphics,
North Mankato, Minnesota

9 8 7 6 5 4 3 2 1

ISBN: 978-1-62588-349-0

# contents

# making a start

The key to drawing well is learning to look carefully. Study your subject till you know it really well. Keep a sketchbook with you and draw whenever you get the chance. Even doodling is good—it helps to make your drawing more confident. You'll soon develop your own style of drawing, but this book will help you to find your way.

Practice drawing stick figures for basic poses.

# quick sketches

Try sketching details from books or magazines.

# perspective

**P**erspective is a way of drawing objects so that they look as though they have three dimensions. Note how the part that is closest to you looks larger, and the part furthest away from you looks smaller. That's just how things look in real life.

The vanishing point (V.P.) is the place in a perspective drawing where parallel lines appear to meet. The position of the vanishing point depends on the viewer's eye level.

V.P.

It can be helpful to use the perspective construction lines to divide the body into different sections. This ensures you get the proportion of each section correct in comparison with each other.

# two-point perspective drawing

Two-point perspective uses two vanishing points: one for lines running along the length of the subject, and one on the opposite side for lines running across the width of the subject.

In this drawing the vanishing points are low. This gives the impression that you are looking up at the figure—very dramatic!

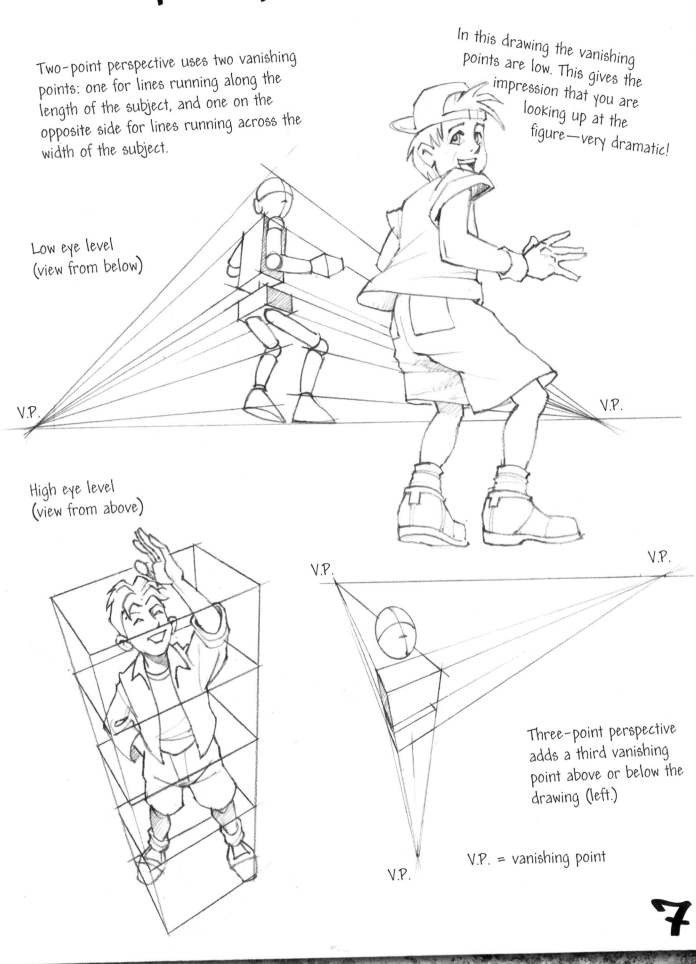

Low eye level
(view from below)

V.P.

V.P.

High eye level
(view from above)

V.P.

V.P.

Three-point perspective adds a third vanishing point above or below the drawing (left.)

V.P.

V.P. = vanishing point

**7**

# materials

Remember, the best equipment and materials will not necessarily make the best drawing—only practice will.

## pencils

Try out different grades of pencils. Hard pencils make fine gray lines and soft pencils make softer, darker marks.

## erasers

are useful for cleaning up drawings and removing construction lines.

## paper

Bristol paper is good for crayons, pastels, and felt-tip pens. Watercolor paper is thicker; it is the best choice for water-based paints or inks.

Use this sandpaper block if you want to shape your pencil to a really sharp point.

8

# inks

Use colored inks straight from the bottle or dilute them with water.

# felt-tip pens

Felt-tips usually come in sets of mixed colors. The ones that make very thin lines are called fineliners.

Ink

Mixing palette

Fineliners

Dip-in pen nibs

Brushes

Correction fluid

Gouache

Watercolors

# pens

Technical drawing pens have cartridges which can be refilled or replaced. Old-fashioned dip-in pens are much cheaper and come in many different styles and sizes.

# paints

Ordinary watercolors are translucent (see-through); gouache is not. Try other kinds of paints, too.

Technical drawing pens

9

# styles

Try different types of drawing papers and materials. Experiment with pens, from felt-tips to ballpoints, and make interesting marks. What happens if you draw with pen and ink on wet paper?

**Silhouette** is a style of drawing which mainly relies on solid dark shapes.

**Felt-tips** come in a range of line widths. The wider pens are good for filling in large areas of flat tone.

10

**Pencil** drawings can include a vast amount of detail and tone. Try different grades of pencil to get a range of light and shade effects in your drawings.

Lines drawn in **ink** cannot be erased, so unless you are very confident you may want to sketch your drawing in pencil first.

It can be tricky adding light and shade to a drawing with a pen. Use a solid layer of ink for the very darkest areas and cross-hatching (straight lines criss-crossing each other) for ordinary dark tones. Use hatching (straight lines running parallel to each other) for midtones.

Hatching          Cross-hatching

# body proportions

**H**eads in manga are drawn slightly bigger than in real life. Legs and hips make up more than half the overall height of the figure.

Drawing a stick figure is the simplest way to make decisions about a pose. It helps you see how different positions can change the center of balance.

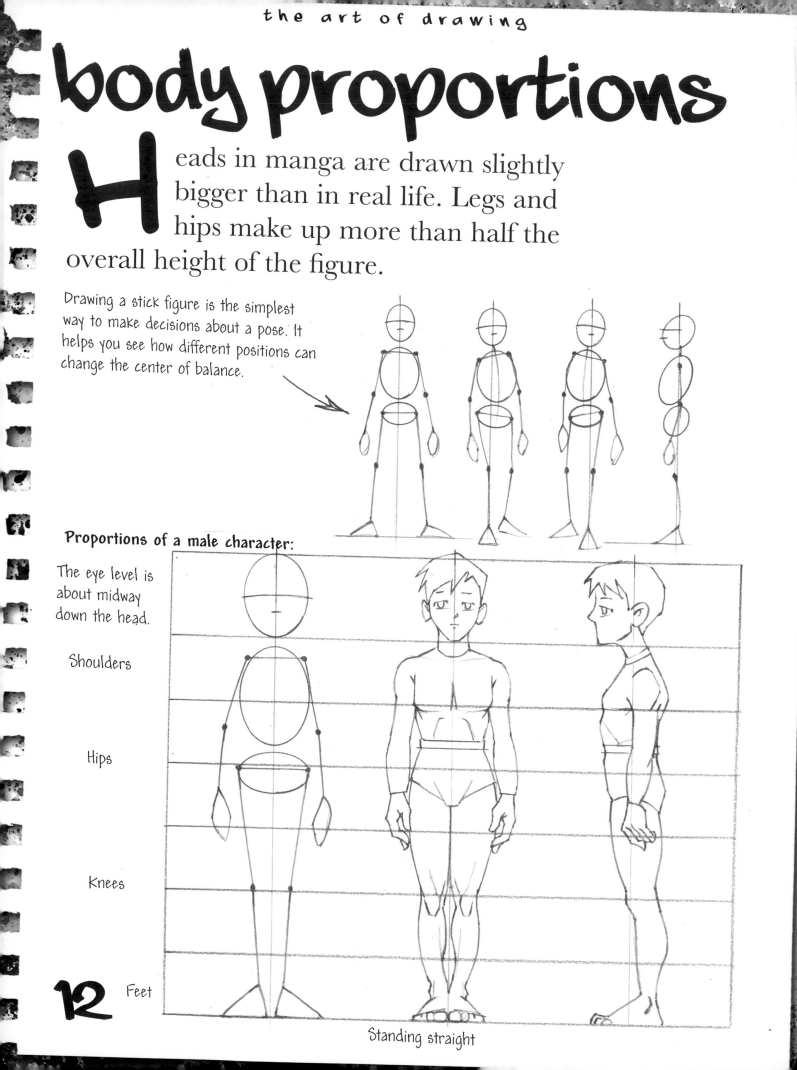

**Proportions of a male character:**

The eye level is about midway down the head.

Shoulders

Hips

Knees

**12** Feet

Standing straight

# inking

Here's one way of inking over your final pencil drawing.

Refillable inking pens come in various tip sizes. The tip is what determines the width of the line that is drawn. Sizes include: 0.1, 0.5, 1.0, 2.0 mm.

Different tones of ink can be used to add depth to the drawing.
Mix ink with water to achieve the tones you need.

Correction fluid usually comes in small bottles or in pen format. This can be useful for cleaning up ink lines.

# heads

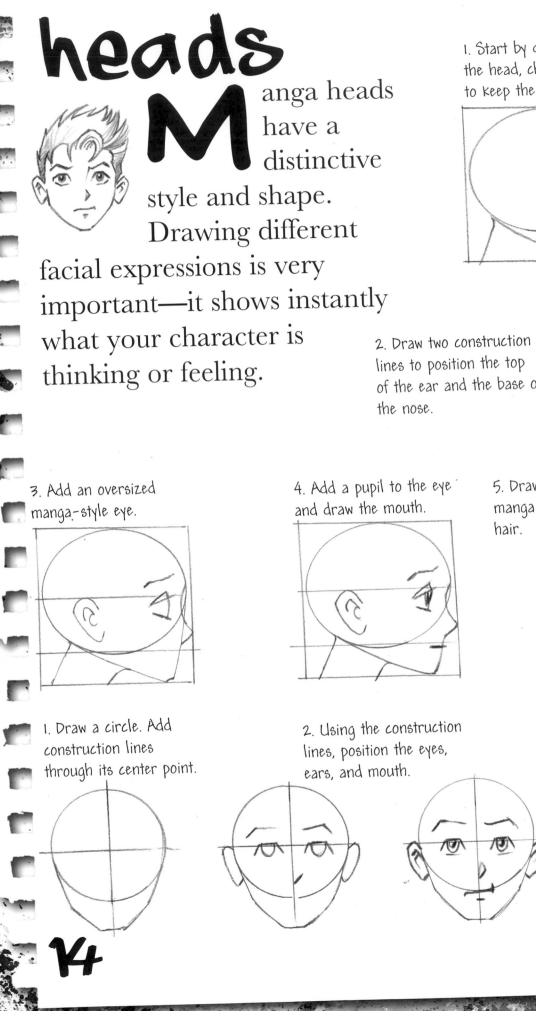

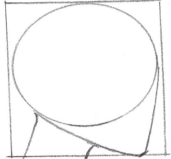

**M**anga heads have a distinctive style and shape. Drawing different facial expressions is very important—it shows instantly what your character is thinking or feeling.

1. Start by drawing a square. Fit the head, chin, and neck inside it to keep the correct proportions.

2. Draw two construction lines to position the top of the ear and the base of the nose.

3. Add an oversized manga-style eye.

4. Add a pupil to the eye and draw the mouth.

5. Draw some manga-style hair.

1. Draw a circle. Add construction lines through its center point.

2. Using the construction lines, position the eyes, ears, and mouth.

3. Draw the hair and add finishing touches.

Practice drawing heads from different angles and with different facial expressions.

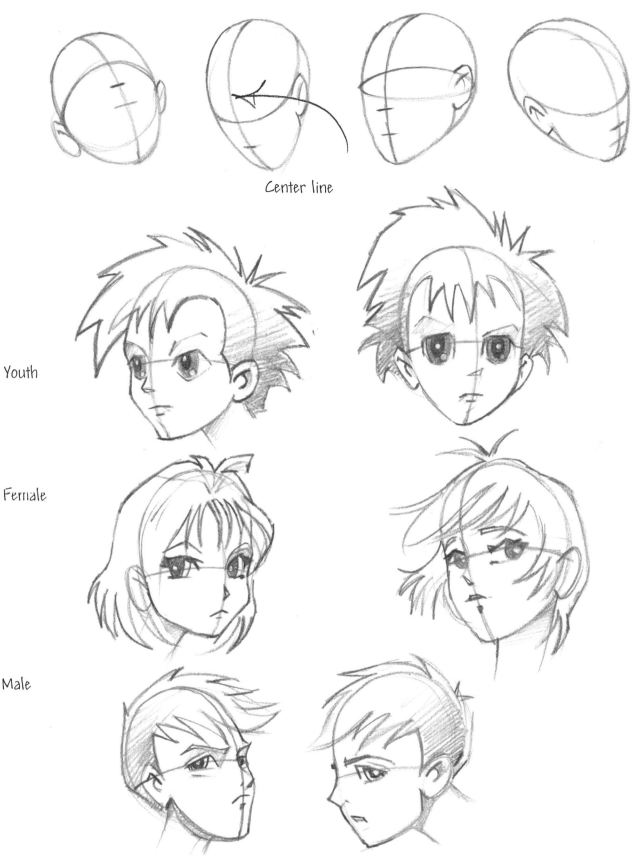

Center line

Youth

Female

Male

Practicing different facial expressions allows you
to explore the personality of your character.

# creases and folds

Clothes fall into natural creases and folds when worn. Look at real people to see how fabric drapes and how it falls into creases. This will help you to dress your characters more realistically.

Creases occur where excess fabric gathers in folds. Drawing creases in clothing at joints will make your picture look more lifelike.

Clothes will hang and crease differently depending on the material.

Drawing from life can help you understand where and why creases and folds occur.

16

The way fabric is drawn can instantly give a sense of movement and action to a pose.

Shading clothes is also very important. Think of all the places the light won't reach, such as inside trouser legs.

Shading in pencil first before adding ink helps avoid mistakes.

17

# skateboarder

T his young boy is a fantastic skateboarder. He can perform all sorts of amazing tricks and jumps at fast speeds.

1. Draw ovals for the head, body, and hips. Add center lines to divide the head vertically and horizontally. These will help you to place the ears and the nose.

2. Add lines for the spine and the angle of the hips and shoulders.

3. Draw stick arms and legs, with dots where the joints are. Add outline shapes for hands and feet.

Start adding in the facial features and hair.

4. Using the construction lines as a guide, add the basic shapes of the body and clothes.

5. Add the basic shape of the skateboard.

These little circles are to remind you where the elbows and knees go.

18

6. Draw the clothes, hair, and facial features. This is where your drawing really starts to come to life.

Add the basic shape of the shirt.

7. If you don't want your construction lines to show, erase them before you do the final shading and details.

Add dark shading to any area light wouldn't reach.

8. Now finish all the little details, such as the details of the clothes, hair, and face, and the shading. Don't rush! The more carefully you do these finishing touches, the better your drawing will look.

Instead of shading your drawing you can try finishing your drawing in ink. Go over all outlines in ink and remove any pencil lines.

# schoolboy

**T**his boy is dressed in a traditional Japanese school uniform called the gakuran.

1. Draw a circle for the head and ovals for the body and hips.

2. Add lines for the spine and the angle of the hips and shoulders.

3. Draw stick arms and legs with dots for the joints and shapes for the hands and feet.

4. Use your guidelines to sketch in the neck, facial features, and hair.

5. Using the construction lines as a guide, start drawing in the main shapes of the body.

Small circles indicate the positions of elbows and knees.

6. Now start to sketch out the final shapes of clothes, hair, arms, and legs.

**20**

7. If you don't want your construction lines to show, erase them carefully before you add the finishing touches: shading, facial features, patterns on the clothes.

8. Complete your drawing adding all the final detail.

Look at how angles in the body create folds in the fabric of the clothes.

Add details to the bag and strap.

Add shading to any areas light wouldn't reach.

If you want a different final look to your drawing you can try finishing it in ink. Carefully go over any outlines and then remove any leftover pencil lines with an eraser.

21

# otaku

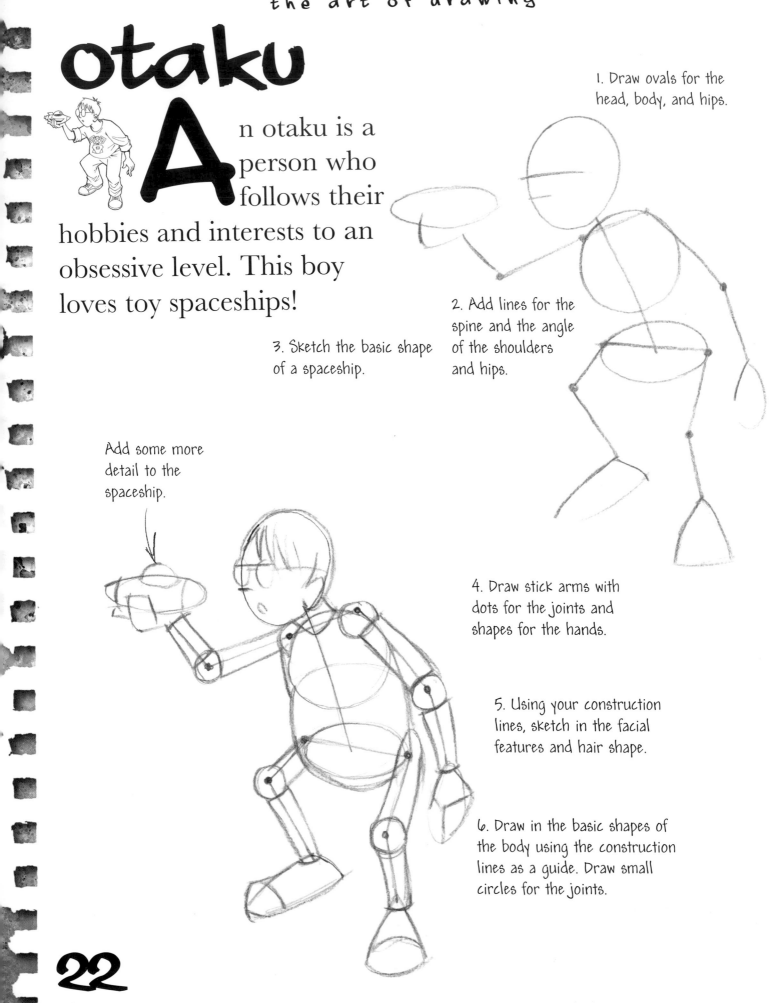

**A**n otaku is a person who follows their hobbies and interests to an obsessive level. This boy loves toy spaceships!

1. Draw ovals for the head, body, and hips.

2. Add lines for the spine and the angle of the shoulders and hips.

3. Sketch the basic shape of a spaceship.

Add some more detail to the spaceship.

4. Draw stick arms with dots for the joints and shapes for the hands.

5. Using your construction lines, sketch in the facial features and hair shape.

6. Draw in the basic shapes of the body using the construction lines as a guide. Draw small circles for the joints.

Add some strands of hair.

7. Draw in the details of the clothes and facial expression.

Add more technical detail to the spaceship.

8. Erase your construction lines if you don't want them to show.

Leave the lenses of the glasses blank to suggest a reflective surface.

You could try finishing your drawing in ink.

9. Complete your drawing, adding final details and shading where necessary.

**23**

# bosozoku leader

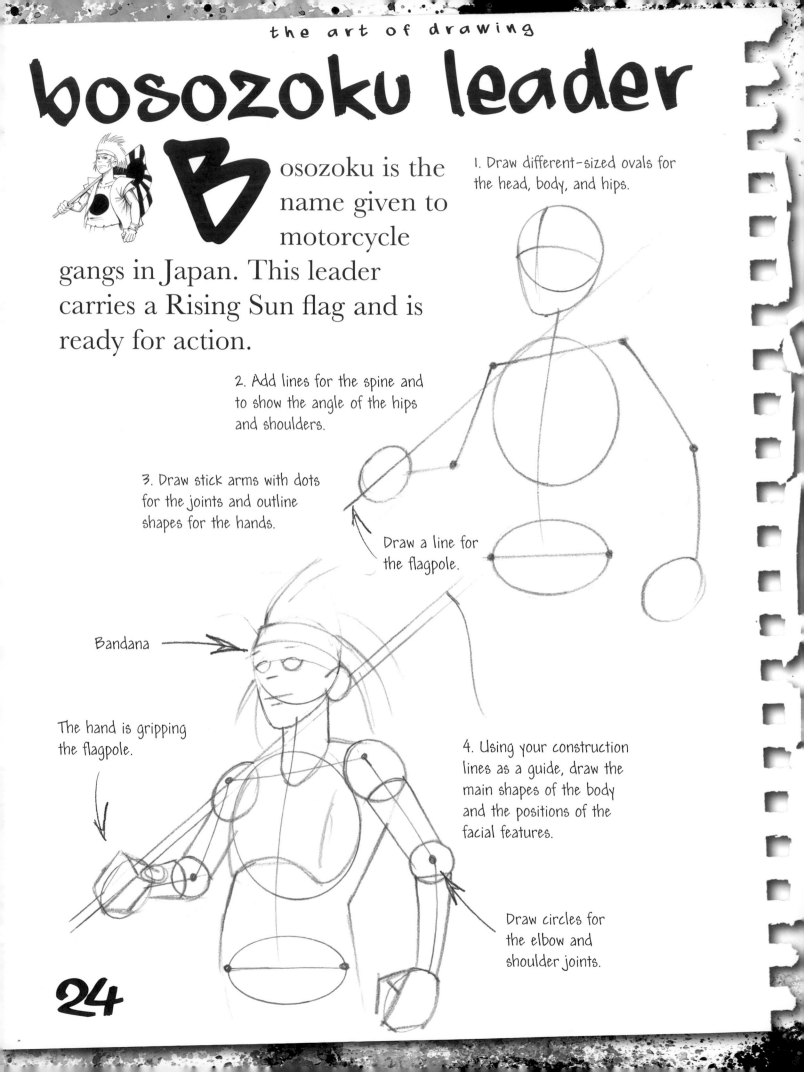

osozoku is the name given to motorcycle gangs in Japan. This leader carries a Rising Sun flag and is ready for action.

1. Draw different-sized ovals for the head, body, and hips.

2. Add lines for the spine and to show the angle of the hips and shoulders.

3. Draw stick arms with dots for the joints and outline shapes for the hands.

Draw a line for the flagpole.

Bandana

The hand is gripping the flagpole.

4. Using your construction lines as a guide, draw the main shapes of the body and the positions of the facial features.

Draw circles for the elbow and shoulder joints.

24

5. Add detail to the face, hair, and costume.

Start to add shade to the darkest areas.

Add the fingers.

6. Erase the construction lines if you want to. Finish off all remaining costume details and add shading.

Shade in the flag design.

Add creases and folds to the fabric.

Draw in the leather glove details.

Go over the main outlines in ink and then erase the pencil drawing underneath for a different outcome.

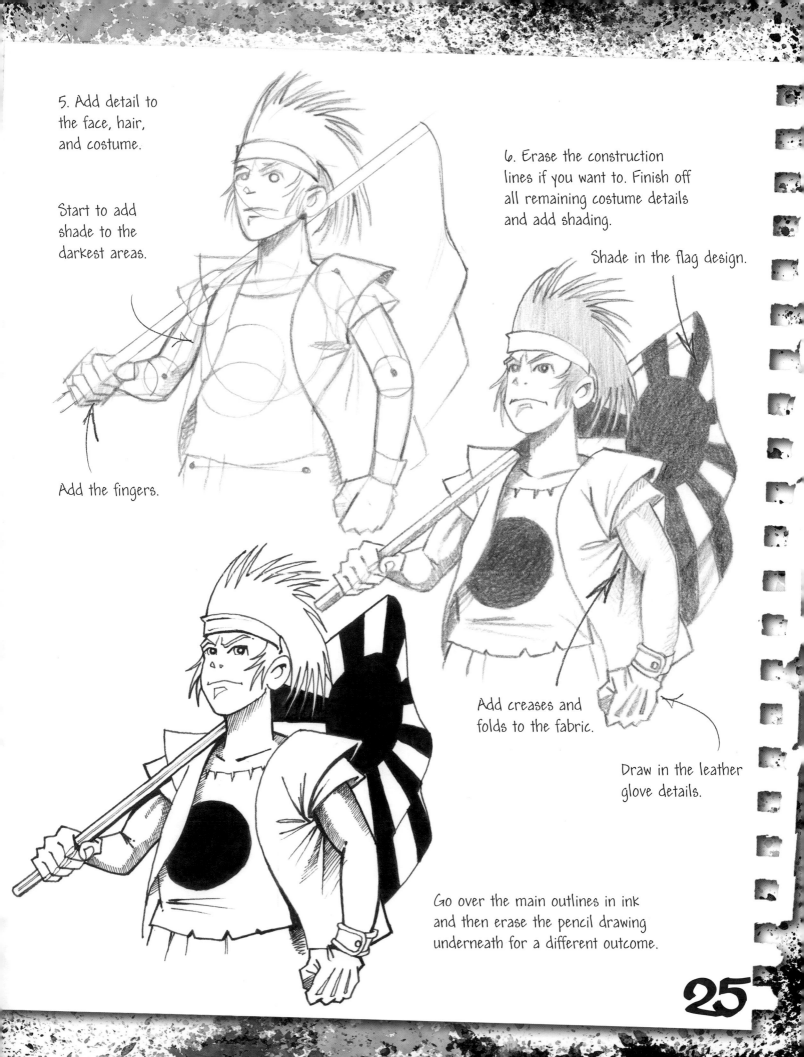

# baseball star

This baseball star is the captain of his school team. His dream is to win the Summer Koshien—the nationwide school baseball championship.

1. Draw ovals for the head, body, and hips.

Add a line for the bat.

2. Add lines for the spine and the angle of the shoulders and hips.

3. Draw stick arms with dots for the joints and shapes for the hands and feet.

The wide legs in this pose give a sense of action.

Sketch in basic facial features and a hat.

4. Draw in tube-shaped arms and legs with circles for the knees and elbows.

Draw in the basic shape of the bat.

Don't forget to use your construction lines as a guide when drawing the basic shapes of the body.

26

5. Start to add detail to the face, body, and clothes.

Add the hat and hair.

Draw in the fingers of the hand gripping the bat.

Draw in lines for the folds in the clothes.

6. Erase the construction lines if you want to.

7. Complete the drawing adding all final details and important shading.

Add shade to areas light wouldn't reach.

The folds and creases in the fabric show how the body is twisting.

You can try finishing your drawing in ink.

Draw in your own baseball gear details.

27

# festival boy

**T**his boy is ready for the New Year's festival wearing a traditional outfit.

1. Draw ovals for the head, body, and hips.

2. Add lines for the spine and to show the angle of the hips and shoulders.

3. Draw stick arms with dots for the joints and shapes for the hands.

Add a line for the baton.

4. Draw in tube-shaped arms and legs with circles for the knees and elbows.

Add the darkest area of shade.

Small circles indicate the positions of elbows and knees.

5. Start to add detail to the face, body, and hands.

28

Draw two white paper streams (shide) coming off the baton.

6. Add more detail to the face and hands, then draw in the clothes around the body.

Short spiky hairstyle.

7. Erase the construction lines if you want to. Finish off all remaining costume details and add shading.

Pay particular attention to the folds and creases of the traditional outfit, taking care to see how they affect the shading.

Here's the same drawing finished in ink.

# boy detective

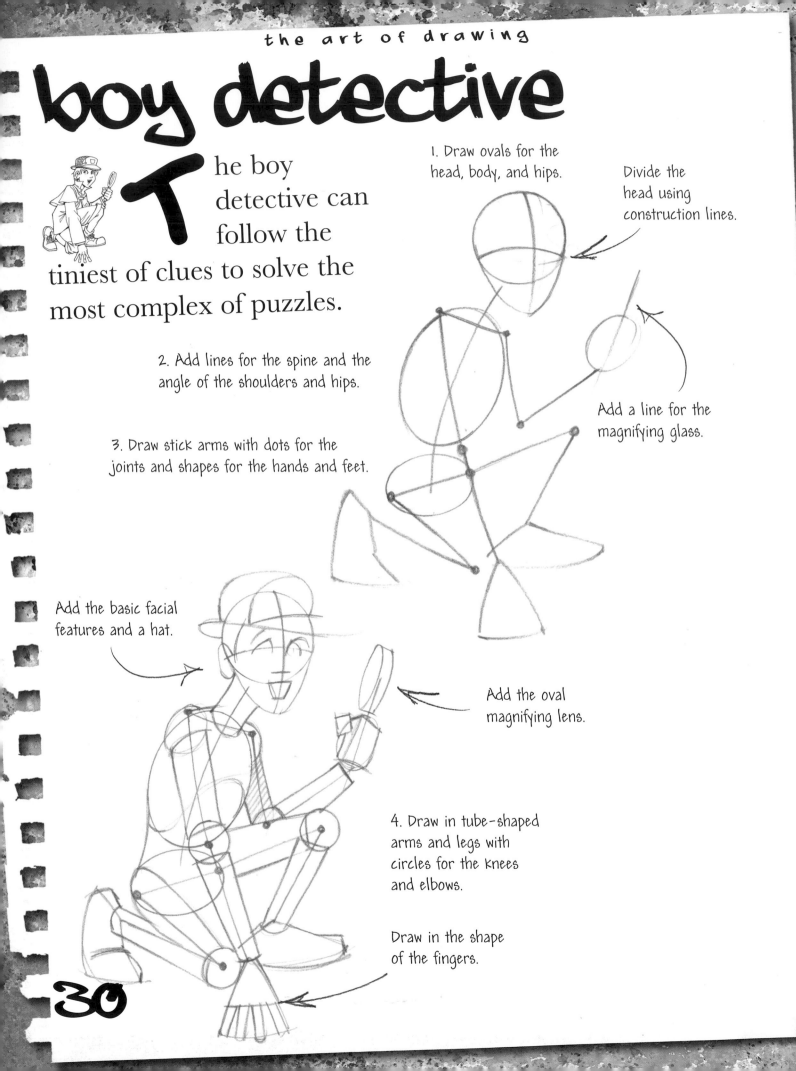

**T**he boy detective can follow the tiniest of clues to solve the most complex of puzzles.

1. Draw ovals for the head, body, and hips.

Divide the head using construction lines.

2. Add lines for the spine and the angle of the shoulders and hips.

Add a line for the magnifying glass.

3. Draw stick arms with dots for the joints and shapes for the hands and feet.

Add the basic facial features and a hat.

Add the oval magnifying lens.

4. Draw in tube-shaped arms and legs with circles for the knees and elbows.

Draw in the shape of the fingers.

30

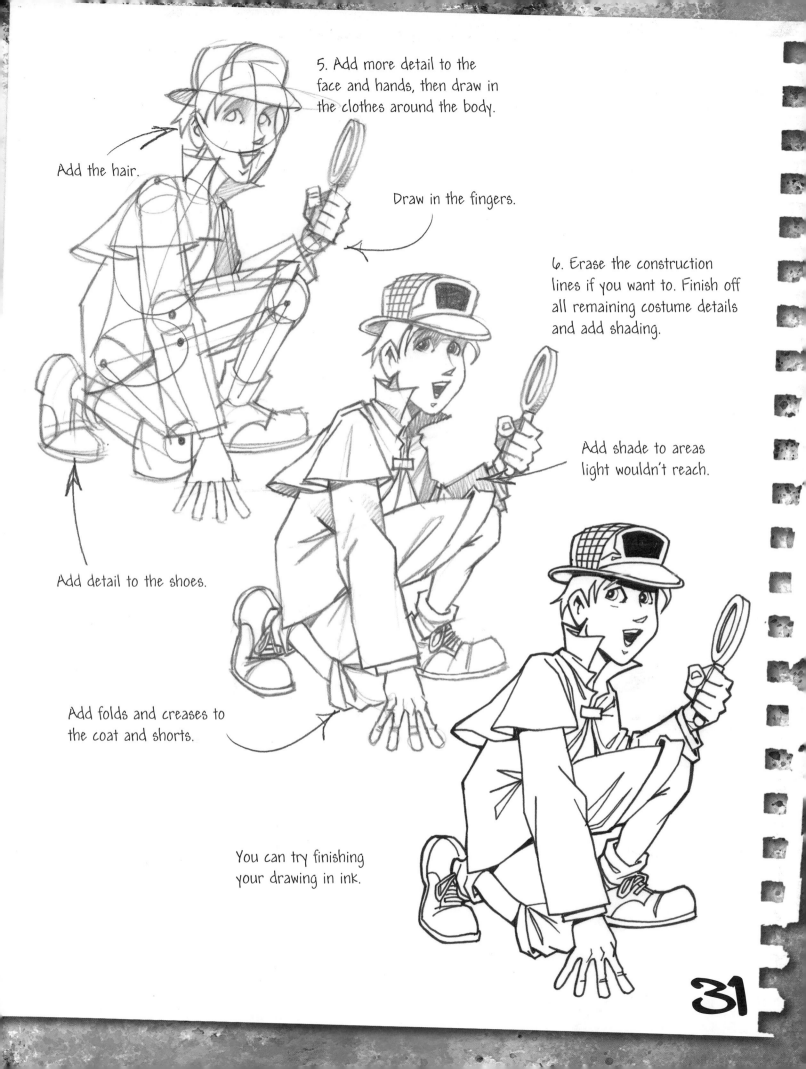

5. Add more detail to the face and hands, then draw in the clothes around the body.

Add the hair.

Draw in the fingers.

6. Erase the construction lines if you want to. Finish off all remaining costume details and add shading.

Add shade to areas light wouldn't reach.

Add detail to the shoes.

Add folds and creases to the coat and shorts.

You can try finishing your drawing in ink.

31

# glossary

**Composition** The positioning of the various parts of a picture on the drawing paper.

**Construction lines** Guidelines used in the early stages of a drawing which are usually erased later.

**Cross-hatching** A series of criss-crossing lines used to add shade to a drawing.

**Hatching** A series of parallel lines used to add shade to a drawing.

*Manga* A Japanese word for "comic" or "cartoon"; also the style of drawing that is used in Japanese comics.

**Silhouette** A drawing that shows only a dark shape, like a shadow, sometimes with a few details left white.

**Three-dimensional** Having an effect of depth, so as to look like a real character rather than a flat picture.

**Tone** The contrast between light and shade that helps to add depth to a picture.

**Vanishing point** The place in a perspective drawing where parallel lines appear to meet.

# index